This is Book Five of

Regeneration Effect :

Sacred Wisdom for Staying Young Keep Your

Life Unobstructed, Follow Nature's Rhythm

BOOK 5

Since childhood, I've been fascinated by the human body—how every system works in harmony to sustain life. I grew up surrounded by its philosophy: the balance of Yin and Yang, the movement of Qi, the interdependence of the Five Elements—all pointing to one truth: health is the result of balance, not simply the absence of disease.

The early masters of Chinese medicine and Taoist philosophy weren't just treating

Keep Your Life Unobstructed, Follow Nature's Rhythm

Dr. Yi Song

Copyright © 2026 Dr. Yi Song

All rights reserved. No part of this book may be reproduced, stored in a retrieval system, or transmitted in any form by any means—electronic, mechanical, photocopying, recording, or otherwise—without written permission from the publisher.

ISBN: 979-8-9948506-6-4 (print)

illness; they were exploring the boundaries

of human life. Through herbal

experimentation, meditation, breath work,

and disciplined living, they sought to extend

vitality indefinitely. Yet, even the greatest

among them could not escape mortality. What they discovered instead was something far more profound: how to live *well* within the natural limits of life. They found that true longevity is not about endless years but about expanding the quality of those years—living in harmony with nature's rhythms, preserving health, and nurturing the mind and spirit.

Modern Life vs. Ancient Rhythm

Aligning with seasonal and cyclical changes Your body doesn't respond the same way in winter as it does in summer.

Hormones, digestion, mood, and metabolism

all shift with the seasons. And with the

stages of life. Learning to work *with* those

changes is key to long-term vitality.

Today's world demands constant

productivity. You're praised for "powering

through," rewarded for exhaustion, and

admired for multi-tasking through burnout.

But this mindset is one of the most

dangerous myths in modern culture.

But nature doesn't operate that way.

Nature doesn't heal through force—it heals through flow.

Water doesn't carve canyons by slamming into rock; it reshapes the world through steady, rhythmic persistence.

Plants don't grow because someone yanks them toward the sun; they unfurl on their own timeline. Even seasons understand this: winter retreats not because spring fights it, but because the natural cycle allows the shift.

Your healing works exactly the same way.

Recovery doesn't start with friction, resistance, or willpower—it begins with allowing.

When you stop fighting your body and start listening to it, you give it permission to recalibrate.

When you slow down, breathe, and create

stillness, you open up the internal space

where repair can happen. Rest isn't passive;

it's one of the most active biological states

your body enters. Hormones rebalance.

Inflammation lowers. Neural pathways reset. Cells detoxify and rebuild.

In earlier ages, humanity lived in closer rhythm with nature. Survival required awareness, intuition, and the ability to sense subtle shifts in environment, emotion, and energy.

That instinctive intelligence still exists within us, but modern life—with its constant stimulation, distraction, and artificial comfort—has softened that

connection. We've replaced presence with screens, emotion with numbness, and internal alignment with external validation.

For many who struggle with addiction—whether alcohol, drugs, or other compulsive behaviors—**the altered state offers something deeper than escape.**

In that intoxication, there is a fleeting feeling of returning to something ancient and instinctual. For a moment, the thinking mind quiets, the nervous system loosens, and the person feels more open, intuitive, and uninhibited. It mimics a state humanity once accessed naturally: internal ease, emotional freedom, a sense of belonging within oneself and the world.

One client described their desire not just to stop drinking, but to access what ancient

Daoist alchemists called the "immortal embryo" (shengtai)—a state of inner purity and original awareness.

Daoist tradition teaches that this state

represents a return to the consciousness of

the fetus: present, unburdened, connected to

source.

In that stage of being, **there is no separation between body, spirit, and the Dao.**

There is only flow.

This may explain why **so many are drawn to intoxication or altered states—not because they are weak, but because they are unconsciously longing for that original innocence:** the unfiltered perception of a child who senses truth, energy, and emotion before language interrupts it. Infants live in this state effortlessly, but they cannot articulate what they feel. As we age, language replaces instinct, expectation replaces curiosity, and logic replaces intuition. The connection fades.

Dependence forms because the shortcut feels easier than the path. Substances offer temporary access to a heightened state, but without true integration. The body remembers the feeling and wants it again, yet the shortcut never brings stability—only repetition. The illusion is compelling: for a moment, one feels expansive, clear, whole.

But because it's chemically produced rather than cultivated, it dissolves quickly, leaving a deeper craving.

Real connection—true presence—cannot be rushed.

If someone seeks that purity of awareness, that sense of inner unity, it requires commitment, practice, and patience.

Meditation, breath work, embodiment

practices, emotional healing, and aligned living build that inner state slowly, but they build it in a way that lasts.

The longing is not the problem. The shortcut is.

If the goal is to return to the instinct, intuition, and spiritual clarity we once held, then the work becomes learning to access those states without external crutches—so that connection is no longer temporary, but lived.

Eastern wisdom teaches that **power comes from alignment, not effort.** Like bamboo, we are strongest when we are rooted in flexibility.

The more you pause and return to center, the more effective your actions become.

The Gift of Pause

We've all had moments where we feel

disconnected from ourselves—burned out,

exhausted, emotionally overwhelmed, or
just... off.

**The instinct, especially for high achievers
or caretakers, is often to *do more*.**

Double the workouts. Tighten the food plan.
Work longer hours. Meditate harder. Push
harder to "fix it." But here's the hard truth:
You can't heal from a stressed state.

When your nervous system is constantly in
fight-or-flight—when you're running on

adrenaline, stress hormones, and pressure—

your body literally can't absorb healing.

· Nutrients don't assimilate.

· Sleep doesn't restore.

· Thoughts can't process clearly.

· Emotions don't integrate.

· Even breath stays shallow, as if your body

is bracing for a storm.

The first, most radical step to resetting your

health is this:

Let go of the grip.

We're exhausted, bloated, irritable, unable to sleep. Our joints ache. Our digestion is a mess. We don't laugh much.

We've been taught to fight against age instead of flow with life. To manage symptoms instead of nurture balance. I'm here to show you ways to keep yourself happy and healthy with the right tools.

Practical Reset Rituals

Resetting doesn't always require a dramatic retreat or a week off. Often, the most powerful resets happen in **micro-moments —small shifts that realign your energy, clarity, and nervous system.**

Below are simple rituals you can return to again and again.

Breath Reset

Your breath is the fastest way to shift your

nervous system out of stress mode and into

calm. Even just **3 minutes** can transform your inner state.

Try this: Sit quietly. Inhale for 4 → Hold for 4 → Exhale for 6. Repeat this for 6 rounds. Let the breath lengthen naturally.

Sleep Reset

One night of deep, unbroken sleep can restore more than a week of stressed-out productivity. Rest isn't a luxury. It's your birthright.

Try this:

· Power down all screens at least two hours before bed.

· Lay on your back and try *legs-up-the-wall* pose for 10 minutes.

· Sip a warm, calming tea like **chamomile**, **tulsi**, or **reishi**.

· Give yourself permission to **fully rest**—without needing to "earn it."

Nutrition Reset

When your digestion is off, your mood, energy, and focus all follow. Your gut is your **second brain**—and it needs simplicity to heal.

Try this:

· For 2–3 days, eat simple, nourishing

meals: Soups, congee, warm cooked

vegetables, bone broth.

· Avoid raw, cold, or complex meals that

stress your digestive fire.

· Add warming herbs like **ginger**,

cinnamon, and **fennel** to support gut

balance.

Mental Reset

Mental clutter drains your energy just like physical exhaustion. Unspoken worries, looping thoughts, and inner criticism create invisible weight.

Try this:

· Write one full page answering: *"What am I holding onto that I'm ready to release?"*

· Speak out loud what you're thinking— naming it gives it less power.

· Visualize your mind like a clear sky, watching thoughts float by like passing clouds.

Qi Reset

Energy (Qi) flows like water. If it gets blocked, symptoms appear: fatigue, pain, brain fog, or emotional swings. QiGong and movement help restore flow.

Try this:

· Practice gentle QiGong for 10 minutes— morning or evening. Movements like

"Swimming Dragon", **"Spinal Shake"**, or **"Cloud Hands"** are beautiful places to start.

· Even a simple **walking meditation** or slow, rhythmic breathing outdoors resets your inner terrain.

You Deserve to Reset

You don't need to collapse before you take rest. You don't need to prove your worth to justify slowing down. The **reset button** is always available—and sometimes, pressing it is the bravest thing you can do.

Reflection Exercise

Take a few moments to reflect or journal on the following:

· Where in your life do you feel **tension**, **resistance**, or **fatigue**?

· What signs is your **body** giving you that something needs to shift?

· What would a **reset** look like for you this week—big or small?

· What **fears or beliefs** do you carry around slowing down? Where did they come from?

Remember: Slowing down is not a step back. It's often the most sacred step forward.

It lives in the way your body wakes up in the morning. In how deeply you sleep. In whether you can climb stairs without wincing. In the sound of your own laughter. In the ability to move, breathe, eat, and feel without discomfort.

That's what matters. That's what lasts.

I once sat on a bench beside an elderly woman in a park in Hangzhou. She must've been in her 80s, maybe even 90s. We spoke for a while, and **I asked her what her secret was.**

She smiled and said, "I walk every morning before the city wakes.

I drink warm tea, eat simple food, never argue. And I listen to birds instead of news."

Then she laughed, stood up, and walked away faster than I expected. That moment stuck with me more than any TED Talk on longevity ever has.

Of course, I've also heard people—especially in the West—say,

"Once you hit 70, it's all downhill.

Doctors, medications, surgeries—that's just life." And I get it. That might be true for many, because it's what we've come to expect.

But that doesn't mean it's inevitable.

Some believe aging is a slow surrender.

I believe aging is a sacred art.

When you embrace the principles the ancients taught—**balance, rest, nourishment, mindfulness**—you give yourself a fighting chance. Not just to live longer, but to live *better*.

So no, I'm not chasing immortality.

I believe in living well, Over living forever.

Fully, intentionally, joyfully—for as long as I can.

If that's 80 years, let them be radiant. If it's 100, let them be free of bitterness and burden. And if I'm lucky enough to touch 120, I hope I still wake up early, drink warm tea, and listen to the birds.

That, to me, is the goal: not eternal life, but meaningful days. Not immortality, but vitality—carried gracefully, one breath at a time.

If you would like more personalized advice

on how to keep your life unobstructed and

follow nature's rhythm, please scan the QR

code for more information to preorder

"Regeneration Effect: Sacred Wisdom for

Staying Young" and learn how you can

implement all the principles in your life.

ABOUT THE AUTHOR

Dr. Yi Song was born and raised in Beijing, China, into a family with seventeen generations of experience in both Chinese and Western medicine. Twenty-eight years ago, she came to the United States to study pathology at Brown University. After observing the shortcomings of symptom-focused treatments, Dr. Song returned to her roots to focus on true regenerative healing — addressing disease at its source. She has had a holistic clinic in Boston since 2004. In

2018, she founded the Zenerchi Retreat in Medellin, Colombia. Her introduction to stem cell therapy in 2020 was marked by her mother's successful treatment and subsequent independence at age 81. Dr. Song believes that stem cell therapy aligns with holistic principles and is the author of "Regeneration Effect: Sacred Wisdom for Staying Young" and the series of seven books in "The Six Principles to Natural Longevity". Her vision is to combine stem cell therapy, Traditional Chinese Medicine, and anti-aging treatments to help people live a long, high-quality life. She offers advanced stem cell treatments at Zenerchi Retreat in Colombia not available in the US. You can also get consultation about your conditions and concerns in person in Boston or at our network of doctors in the US and online.

www.ingramcontent.com/pod-product-compliance
Lightning Source LLC
Chambersburg PA
CBHW040900110726
48005CB00001B/142